TESTAMENT OF SOLOMON

RECENSION C

Testament of Solomon (recension C) © Brian Johnson, 2019
Foreword © David Rankine
Images © S. Aldarnay
Reproduced from Harley MS 5596 and Parisinus Graec. MS 2419
All Rights Reserved.
This softcover edition ISBN 978 1 907881 94 7
Standard edition of 120 copies bound in amethyst cloth.
Typeset in Alfios.
Published by Hadean Press.
West Yorkshire

www.hadeanpress.com

TESTAMENT OF SOLOMON

RECENSION C

*An Original Translation
with Annotations and Commentary*

BRIAN JOHNSON

CONTENTS

FOREWORD

The *Testament of Solomon* is hugely important in the grimoire tradition, one of the progenitor texts which influenced the corpus of material that would follow on. As H.M. Jackson observed *"The Testament of Solomon and all the tracts of its kindred genres in occult science - herbals, lapidaries, bestiaries, and the like - were living texts"*.[1]

Like the grimoires which would descend from it, the *Testament of Solomon* was formed over centuries and across countries, accreting wisdom like a pearl, and shining forth into our current age. A living text such as the *Testament of Solomon* contains a vitality of truth, which is ageless and eternally relevant. In producing this excellent commented scholarly translation, Brian Johnson displays this pearl for all to behold.

The importance of this early spirit list of demons, and significantly, their controlling angels, cannot be overstated. When reading this book, I would urge the reader to pay equal attention to the extensive footnotes, which provide a wealth of context and material that expand the scope of the work.

The author's research supports the idea of the development of much of the grimoire tradition from early Greek and Jewish magic, discussed by Stephen Skinner and myself in *The Veritable Key of Solomon* (2008); and I am confident it will provide another stepping stone on the path to a fuller and richer understanding of the grimoire tradition.

David Rankine

---

1 "Notes on the Testament of Solomon", H.M.Jackson, *Journal for the Study of Judaism* Vol 19.1.19

INTRODUCTION

The *Testament of Solomon* (hereafter *TSol*) is not just one text, or even precisely one story. It is, rather, a handful of distinct narratives, often overlapping, recounted in manuscripts written hundreds of years and thousands of miles apart, each imagining in its own way and for its own ends the true and complete story of King Solomon – his piety and hubris, humility and ambition; his insight and foolishness; his power, lust, and fall. While these narratives generally agree on the broad outline – Solomon's prayer to God is answered with the power to suborn demons, whom he then systematically interrogates and utilizes as manual laborers – they frequently differ in the precise cast of characters, sequence of scenes, and ultimate fate of the protagonist. The *TSol* is also, and essentially so for its own understanding of Solomon's accomplishments and the nature of his God-given wisdom, a work of practical demonology, with this aspect too adapting to reflect the practical aims of each of its authors no less than their respective cosmologies.

TEXTUAL GENESIS AND MANUSCRIPT TRADITION

Chester Carlton McCown identified three substantively different recensions of the *TSol* – A, B, and C – represented in varying degrees of completeness amongst more than a dozen manuscripts.[1] The most recent translation of the *TSol* into English, by D.C. Duling, is based upon an 'eclectic text' reconstructed by McCown from material in each of the three recensions which he judged to best approximate the hypothetical urtext from which they derived.[2]

To untangle the composition and transmission history of the *TSol* is a vexed undertaking. Scholars have long argued over precisely when, where, and by whom the earliest form of something recognizable as the *TSol* may have been written.[3] Significant elements are attributable to Egyptian sources, and parallels can be found from Palestine to Asia Minor.[4] While evidence within its major textual exemplars betrays a definite Christian influence, external attestations of something called a 'Testament of Solomon' suggest a *terminus ante quem* in the late fourth century CE.[5] McCown adduces a number of legendary Persian figures whose narratives would contribute to the Talmudic image of Solomon, certain pivotal elements of which, including the denouement, are lacking in the Testament.[6] Notwithstanding some indirect Avestan borrowings (e.g. Asmodeus < aēšma-daēva, textually unattested but suggested by parallel forms, as well as *Aēšma* 'wrath' itself

---

1 McCown, 1922
2 Duling, 1983
3 See e.g. Duling, 1988: 88-91
4 Duling, 1988: 96-7
5 Duling, 1983: 955-6
6 McCown, 1922: 55-6

personified as a daeva),[7] this would seem to support a pre-Talmudic date of composition for the *TSol*. It is far from certain, however, that any of these data correspond to one and the same text; it is quite probable that pieces of what would become the *TSol* circulated independently for hundreds of years, gradually accreting around a fixed narrative frame delineating King Solomon's story arc.[8] In addition to its Christian allusions, the demonology and angelology of the *TSol* evince origins in the late-antique synthesis of Egyptian, Hellenic, and Jewish cosmologies and magic.

For instance, in *TSol* II.4 the demon Ornias claims descent from an archangel, and the verb used, ἀπόγονος, implies the genealogical sense. This seems to be an allusion to the Enochic tradition wherein demons are the offspring of fallen angels and mortals. Conversely, we later meet Onoskelis ('she with ass's legs'), who claims to receive worship as some kind of pagan astral goddess, possibly corresponding to the constellation Capricorn.[9] In *TSol* IV.6 she claims to "...associate with men... whose skin is honey-colored...", with whom she shares "...the same constellation" and who "...worship my star secretly and openly". The second-century CE astrologer Claudius Ptolemy, for one, attributed a ruling zodiac sign to each of the world's geographic regions, with Capricorn falling broadly over the southern parts of Eurasia,[10] and in light of Onoskelis's physiognomic predilection it seems plausible that the *TSol* author has a particular pagan *ethnos* in mind here.

Despite its apparent ecumenism and the cosmopolitan milieu in which it probably originated, the *TSol* as it has come down to the present, in a handful of manuscripts dating no earlier than the fifteenth century CE, bears the marks of some ten-hundred years of Christian hegemony. Asmodeus's boasting in *TSol* V.5

7 McCown, 1922: 55 n. 4

8 Schwarz, 2007

9 Duling, 1983: 965 n. 4c

10 *Tetrabiblos* II.iii

implicitly identifies the cosmic gods of pagan antiquity with the *TSol*'s half-angelic demons, and the implicit demonological theory of the text situates the astrologically-predicated illness demons of the broader ancient Near Eastern milieu within a specifically Christianized Judaic cosmological hierarchy of God, Jesus, and the angels. It is quite helpful in this regard that the texts of all extant recensions of the *TSol* are in the Greek language, which allows for a consistent analysis on the basis of specific terminology used therein. While the word πνευμα is occasionally applied to the beings interrogated by Solomon, they are much more frequently determined with some inflection of δαιμων, an equally ambivalent term, but one the valences of which are perhaps more strongly tied to cultural context. Besides the obvious Jewish and Christian scriptural setting of the narrative, most of the demons who are explicitly ascribed a provenance are in one way or another situated within a Biblically-grounded cosmology, and so δαίμων takes on the negative significations of the word in that tradition. While the nature of some, such as the στοιχεία, or decans, remains ambiguous, none of the demons in the *TSol* evince the kind of elevated nature attached to the lemma δαίμων by Homer or Plato.[11] It is for this reason that I have chosen to refer to the beings interrogated by Solomon in the *TSol* as 'demons' rather than daemons, *daimones*, etc., as the modernized form of the word seems to best capture the connotations most probably intended by the authors.

As further evidence of the *TSol*'s Christian biases, consider the parts of rec. C preserved in Bononiensis Uni. MS 3632 and Parisinus Graec. MS 2419, which employ what appears to be a recurring appeal to the authority of King David over and against that of Solomon himself. This is a rhetorical strategy not evinced in those manuscripts preserving other versions of the narrative, either independently or, as in Harley 5596, juxtaposed with parts of rec. C, so this is interesting in its own right as evidence of the ontological

---

11 See Collisson in Skinner, 2010: 42-5

coherence of rec. C across its disparate exemplars. The incipit to the text found in the Bologna and Paris manuscripts specifies that it was after the death of King David that the Testament was kept under guard by Hezekiah ["...ὑπό τοῦ Ἐζεκίου μετά τό ἀποθανεῖν τόν Δαυείδ τόν βασιλέαν ἐφυλάχθησαν"], even though this would be self-evident on the basis of simple Biblical chronology. Likewise, the prologue subordinates Solomon's prayer for divine illumination to the earlier prayer by which David made explicit his wishes for his son: "...μετά τό ἀποθανεῖν τόν Δαυείδ... προσευξαμένου τοῦ υἱοῦ αὐτοῦ οἰκοδομεῖν τήν Σιών...". And the explicit of Bononiensis Uni. MS 3632 reiterates that the Testament which preserves the secret wisdom imparted to Solomon – and what he did with it – was both written and hidden away after David had died. One might well infer that the author here is actually attempting to distance David from culpability for Solomon's ultimate downfall into idolatry, as well as any morally problematic demonology in which his son may have engaged. But at the same time, the text also wishes to emphasize his foundational vision for the city which would be his legacy, even if Solomon did use enslaved demons to build it. Why is the author so invested in David's reputation? The *TSol* as such, all of its Jewish and pagan elements notwithstanding, was even in its earliest iterations the product of a Christianizing milieu, incorporating clear allusions to Christian eschatology and Gospel narratives, and this inclination would only increase in later recensions as the context of composition became – well before the fifteenth century – thoroughly and compulsively Christian. That being the case, the author of rec. C may have been inclined to commemorate David as a particular apogee in the patrilineage of Christ, as attested in the Gospels, while also defending him from direct association with the sins of his progeny. One might even infer an implicit endorsement of the genealogy in Luke 3 which, in contrast to that in Matthew 1, cuts Solomon out of the ancestry of Jesus entirely!

THE DEMONOLOGIST'S RECENSION

Appended to McCown's edition of the Greek text is a substantial portion of rec. C which McCown thought sufficiently interesting to preserve on its own merits, even if it was of little relevance to a reconstruction of the *urtext* and came, in his opinion, "...from a class of men of rather low mentality and poor Greek education".[12] Who were these 'men of low mentality'? Evidently, they were magicians. Indeed, the very text of rec. C which McCown excluded from consideration for his reconstruction, yet found compelling enough to publish, comprises an abundance of elements which set it apart as something more than a work of moralizing Biblical apocrypha and closer to a practicing demonologist's *vade mecum*. This text represents a less-than-seamless interpolation of something approaching the content of many later grimoires, including a unique catalogue of fifty-two demons and the implicit outlines of a ritual methodology by which to command them, into the overarching narrative of the *TSol*. This rec. C material is represented in three manuscripts, Harley 5596, Bononiensis Uni. 3632 and Parisinus Graec. 2419, each of which appears to have been composed in an Italianate milieu at one time or another in the fifteenth century.[13] It comprises alternative versions of the Prologue and chapters IX.8-XIII.15.

This brings us to the work at hand, and the justification for this, the first English translation, collation, and analysis of the text in question. Despite its inherent curiosity and potential value to scholarship on the history of magical theory and practice, no one has heretofore undertaken to make this textual

---

12 McCown, 1922: 36

13 Marathakis, 2011: 18, 20, 22, 75; McCown, 1922: 27

unit accessible to an audience that has not mastered a somewhat archaic form of the Greek language. I have attempted, therefore, with the present translation to do just that. It is my hope that this translation will prove a fruitful object of study for contemporary magical practitioners as well as scholars of intellectual history, Byzantine culture, and many other fields; the following analysis and discussion may suggest several points of departure for further inquiry. I also feel it incumbent upon myself as an inheritor of the intellectual tradition represented in this text to restore a voice to the individuals who composed, copied, and consulted it, as well as to bear witness to the spirits with whom, in one way or another, they made contact.

RECENSION C IN RELATION TO THE GREEK TRADITION OF SOLOMONIC MAGIC

In one of the many colorful episodes of the *TSol*, XX.12-17, the demon Ornias reveals that the demons acquire their knowledge of future events by flying up to the firmament to spy on God's counsels, only to become exhausted and physically plummet like shooting stars back down to earth. In (pseudo?-)Michael Psellos's dialogue *Περι Ενεργειας Δαιμονων* (*De Operatione Daemonum, or On the Operation of Daemons*), Thracian, the better-informed interlocutor and authorial stand-in, asserts that demons do indeed have such bodies,[14] "...which one may learn even from the holy fathers of our religion, if one only addict himself heartily to magical practices".[15] The suggestion here seems to be of some patristic or patriarchal teaching bearing upon the nature of demons, which would only be familiar to practicing magicians. That the author of *Περι Ενεργειας Δαιμονων* was familiar with the *TSol* is strongly suggested by the numerous parallels which can be drawn between the descriptions of demons interrogated by Solomon in the *TSol*, and the characteristics cited in delineating the typological classification of unclean spirits in *Περι Ενεργειας Δαιμονων*.[16] On the other hand, the so-called *Magical Treatise of Solomon*, or *Hygromanteia*, is generally regarded as the prototypical text for a tradition of demonic magic authorizing itself in the name of a Biblical

---

14 The corporeality of demons was orthodox Christian dogma during the first few centuries of the Church, with no less an authority than Augustine espousing the theory, but had fallen out of favor under the influence of Pseudo-Dionysius around the sixth century CE (O'Neill, 2017).

15 Collisson in Skinner, 2010: 61

16 Jackson, 1988: 28 ff.

patriarch,[17] and the earliest extant manuscripts thereof date to the fifteenth century. The evidence for attributing Περι Ενεργειας Δαιμονων to Michael Psellos is ambiguous and disputed,[18] but the work must antedate 1488-9 when Marsilio Ficino was translating it into Latin, albeit no earlier than the flourit of the genuine Psellos in the mid-eleventh century. This being the case, the passage in question seems to be either a roughly contemporary attestation to something very much like those fifteenth-century *Magical Treatise* manuscripts, or else the author is classifying some text in the vein of the *TSol* as a work of practical magic, which could suggest that contemporary practitioners were using it as just that. Indeed, if the *TSol* could be construed as a work of operative magic in the same era that produced the *Magical Treatise*, then it is wholly consistent that an especially demonographic recension of the *TSol* should be bound together with that very same operative work, which is just what we find in Harley MS 5596.

Thracian demurs when pressed to recount the demons' "... names, their forms, and their haunts...",[19] but his very claim to have received such an enumeration suggests the author's familiarity, if only through hearsay, with such demonological catalogues as are found in the Solomonic literature. Likewise, his recommendation that one might cow these demons by invoking "...the angels who are usually despatched against them..."[20] is the very method detailed throughout the *TSol*, to say nothing of the Magical Treatise and its derivatives.

As an aside, circumstantial evidence scattered throughout the oeuvre of Michael Psellos suggests that it would not have been out of character for him to have written a tract like Περι Ενεργειας Δαιμονων. The worldly, learned, but consistently condemnatory

17 Skinner, 2013: 126 ff.
18 Skinner, 2010: 22, but cf. 14
19 Collisson in Skinner, 2010: 64
20 Collisson in Skinner, 2010: 79-80

and reticent account of traffic with demons presented therein seems wholly congruent with the approach to discussing occult topics evinced as much in Psellos's autobiographical reflections as in texts he composed for his students.[21] Conversely, the very initiative to produce such a work is suggestive of Psellos's avowed sense of pedagogical duty to entertain the curiosity of those who earnestly approached him.[22]

Nicetas Acominatus, an official at the Byzantine court in the late twelfth century, wrote of his contemporary, Isaac Aaron, that upon his arrest in 1172 he was found to have in his possession a "book of Solomon which expounded and detailed the legions of demons assembled and standing by whensoever they are called, and who hasten to complete commands and readily respond to orders".[23] As McCown notes, the language here is in some details virtually identical to that found in rec. C concerning the demons' obedience. The existence of texts analogous to rec. C by the middle of the twelfth century would support the ascription of an early date (if not Psellos's authorship per se) to $\Pi\epsilon\rho\iota$ $E\nu\epsilon\rho\gamma\epsilon\iota\alpha\varsigma$ $\Delta\alpha\iota\mu o\nu\omega\nu$, with its apparent allusion to operative Solomonic magic. Moreover, this suggests that rec. C itself, as extant in its fifteenth-century manuscripts, represents a novel appropriation and repurposing of the *TSol* tradition's essential elements, taking into account and reincorporating developments of a more explicitly operative-magical nature that had been modeled upon the *TSol*'s core narrative over the centuries since its initial composition.

Sarah Schwarz has pointed out that the earliest extant material evidence for any part of the *TSol* tradition is a fifth- or sixth-century CE papyrus fragment transmitting chapter XVIII.27-28 and 33-40, part of Solomon's interrogation of thirty-six demons corresponding to the zodiacal decans. The dialogue

21 Duffy, 1995: 88
22 Duffy, 1995: 94
23 My paraphrased translation of the Greek text in McCown, 1922: 102

in this chapter is much more formulaic than that in most of the surrounding narrative, and Schwarz suggests on grounds of form as well as content that it likely circulated as an independent text before eventually being redacted into what would become the *TSol*.[24] At first glance, the roster of fifty-two demons in rec. C may appear even more starkly divorced from its surrounding narrative than does the list of decans. The demons here don't even speak for themselves as others in the *TSol* do, but are instead formulaically described in the third person. Yet upon more careful consideration, the list as a unit plays a much greater structuring role relative to the remainder of rec. C's narrative than the roll of decans does in its own setting. Throughout chapter XII, Paltiel Tzamal repeatedly refers to the demons having written and handed over their own names to Solomon, exactly as promised in IX.10, where the pact's fulfillment is outlined and the content of the list set out. And in XIII Paltiel refers to the list itself as the μυστήριον and θησαυρόν of the Testament, precisely the terms Solomon had used at its conclusion in X.53. I suggest that the list of fifty-two demons, far from being arbitrarily inserted in order to bulk out an otherwise slim work of pseudepigrapha, is in fact the original goetic[25] core around which material from the by-then classic *TSol* narrative was later wrapped sometime in the fifteenth century in order to provide a literary context for its transmission. Indeed, McCown noted that some parts of the manuscript fragment containing the list are written in a form of Greek "...much more modern..." than that of the list itself.[26]

24 Schwarz, 2007: 219

25 I use the term 'goetic' advisedly. While doctrinaire theologians and jurists of the Palaeologan era were prone to conflating the categories of magical practice, all of which they denounced as sources of sinful delusion, it was not unknown for the more learned to distinguish μαγεία from γοητεία, with the latter fairly uniformly held to employ earthly, material, and probably rather corrupt demons (Greenfield 1995: 118-20, and n. 4); a fair characterization of the beings introduced in the *TSol*, even if its author most likely would not have chosen a self-designation so pejorative as γόης.

26 McCown, 1922: 19

The conjurations of the four quarters in the *Magical Treatise* replicate at least nineteen of the demons named in various parts of the *TSol*, including members of the decan spirits as well as individuals interrogated throughout the narrative.[27] This demonstrates two things: first, the coordinated circulation of the *TSol* and *Magical Treatise* from a relatively early point in the redaction history of the latter. The relevant conjurations appear in at least six manuscripts of the *Magical Treatise*, of which at least two dating as early as the sixteenth century (Gennadianus MS 45 and Atheniensis MS 1265) preserve no part of the *TSol* itself. This shows that, less than a century after the composition of our earliest extant manuscripts preserving any coherent form of either the *Magical Treatise* or *TSol*, newly composed exemplars of the *Magical Treatise* separate from any *TSol* text were including material evidently originating in the *TSol* tradition. Second, this pervasive borrowing only further highlights the autonomy of the list of fifty-two demons appearing in the segment of *TSol* rec. C in Harley MS 5596. That manuscript also preserves the *Magical Treatise* with conjurations of the quarters, but with the exception of Astarōth in the west, none of the demons named in these conjurations, nor those appointed to the planets and planetary hours elsewhere in the Harley *Magical Treatise* manuscript, bear more than a remote onomastic resemblance to any of the fifty-two in rec. C. This is further evidence that these latter names are not derived from the 'orthodox' *TSol* canon, but rather represent an independent demonological tradition which has appropriated the *TSol* narrative to itself.

The purely functional exposition and frequently beneficent occupations of the demons enumerated in rec. C stand in contradistinction to those encountered throughout the *TSol*'s primary narrative arc, for whom malefaction is their *raison d'etre*

---

27 All discussion herein of the textual details of the *Magical Treatise* refers to the edition by Marathakis, 2011.

and productive labor only an incidental result of their subjugation. Whereas these latter draw upon an ancient Mesopotamian heritage of personified afflictions, and the spirits listed in grimoires contemporaneous with rec. C, including even the *Magical Treatise* with which it shares Harley MS 5596, are often nothing more than names devoid of character, the fifty-two demons profiled in rec. C have much more in common with later spirit catalogues like those found in Folger MS V.b.26 or the *Livre des esperitz* of Trinity College MS O.8.29, f°s 179-182v°, or indeed with the attributes of planetary and aerial spirits delineated in the *Liber Juratus*, a significantly senior grimoire of the Latin tradition.[28] This suggests that the author of rec. C, if not in fact independently innovating this form of demonological exposition, was drawing upon some as-yet unattested early exemplar(s) of the genre.

The very lack of any evident genealogical relation between the spirit list of rec. C in Harley MS 5596 and that of a text like the aforementioned Folger manuscript, a Latinate grimoire from approximately a century later, is interesting in its own right as an indication of the plurality of textual lineages within Solomonic demonology. Moreover, all of the names which bear even a remote etymological resemblance from one manuscript to the other differ almost obstinately in their descriptive content. The spirits of the Folger manuscript evince greater (which is to say, any) characterization than their Harleian counterparts, yet much more frequent duplication of one another's powers and less functional distinction. The Folger also includes over twice as many names as rec. C, probably drawn from a greater number of sources. If we may hypothesize roughly contemporaneous sources for their respective catalogues, then perhaps this divergence in presentation is simply the result of diachronic processes of artistic elaboration and utilitarian homogenization within the work of scribal transmission and editorial redaction being given two or three generations more

28 See Harms and Peterson, 2015, Boudet, 2003, and Peterson, 2009, respectively.

to operate in the formation of the Folger manuscript than in that of the elder Harley.

Attestations of Solomon's command over demons in texts from the Nag Hammadi corpus (third or fourth century CE); *suwar* 21, 34, and 38 of the Quran (seventh century CE); the Babylonian Talmud (achieving its final form by the beginning of the eighth century CE); and the Cairo Genizah (ninth century CE and later) reflect the pervasiveness, continuity, and power as a cultural touchstone of this aspect of his mythos. As early as the first century BCE, among the Greek Magical Papyri, we find methods of practical enchantment which cite or invoke Solomon.[29] The creative genesis of some such operations may even lie in the mimetic imperative of the Solomonic mythos itself, the attractive power of which was multiplied by the very reproduction of its texts. These Solomonic magical texts would circulate independently, periodically adapted by practitioners to address new situations and emergent exigencies, or incorporated wholesale into miscellaneous compilations. Eventually, somewhere in the Greek-speaking Mediterranean, probably within living memory of Constantinople's fall to the Ottomans if not before, one such text – a roster of demons over whom one could exercise divinely-conferred authority just as King Solomon had once done – was rediscovered by our anonymous magician-scribe. Perhaps found inserted more or less haphazardly within what had been the personal workbook of another practitioner whose name is also lost to history, the text was recognized by our redactor as a long-lost piece of the Solomonic corpus – or at least something easily conformable thereto. The mythic narrative surrounding that textual tradition, attested in a number of forms extant around this same period, might then naturally suggest itself as the most felicitous vehicle by which to transmit this ἀρχαία σοφία. This is not dissimilar to a hypothetical process of redaction which has

---

29 e.g. *PGM* IV.850-929, XCII.1-16

been suggested by several scholars for the *TSol* in general, as noted above.[30]

The fragments of rec. C found in Harley MS 5596 are situated alongside a substantial segment of rec. A, as well as a version of the *Magical Treatise*, in such a way as to raise a number of questions about the editor's intent. First, it quickly becomes clear that the *TSol* material in this manuscript is, in its entirety, structured toward the pragmatic ends of a practicing exorcist, to an extent sometimes not recognized even by the translator of McCown's composite text – to say nothing of McCown's own omissions of esoteric material due to his, perhaps forgivable, incomprehension thereof.[31] Even those segments of the text which otherwise largely correspond to the narrative of rec. A have been found to interpolate explicit instructions of a medico-magical nature, with the prospective reader assuming the role of Solomon himself, and his patient's affliction identified with one of *TSol*'s demons.[32] In terms of its internal organization, the manuscript places rec. C, XI.1-6, the interrogation of the demon Onoskelis, before the main narrative of A, despite the obvious incoherence this creates. Then, after a segment of the manuscript containing the bulk of the *Magical Treatise* material, comes rec. C, IX.8-10, the dialogue in which the demons are promised to Solomon and the ritual implements for their subjugation are prepared, and X.1-52, the demonic roster itself. This is immediately juxtaposed with part of the *Magical Treatise* comprising a long list of angels and demons corresponding to each hour of each day of the week. The text gives no explicit instructions here for interacting with these beings, which suggests – if we set aside for a moment the very real possibility of simple editorial omission – at least two plausible hypotheses: 1) The redactor intended the ritual instructions

30 Alexander and Harding, 1999; Schwarz, 2007

31 Jackson, 1988: 21-2

32 Jackson, 1988: 20 ff.

detailed in the earlier *Magical Treatise* segment, ff. 18v-39v, to apply in working with any and all spirits referred to throughout the codex, in which case the dialogue in rec. C, IX could be read as a dramatized abridgment thereof. Or, 2) the explicit instructions in the *Magical Treatise* and the dialogue in the Testament represent two distinct (albeit obviously related) methodologies, with the list of horary angels and demons subsumed under the same ritual complex as the fifty-two demons of the Testament with whom they form a textual continuum in the manuscript.

Rec. C makes reference in the course of its narrative, albeit not in any systematic way, to a number of ritual implements and prescriptions incumbent upon one who would command the demons named therein; specifically, parchment made from the skin of an unborn animal and inscribed with the sigils and signatures of those demons, a black goat-horn handled knife, and a three-day period of self-purification. Several of these elements are typical of magical operations in the Hellenic tradition, some dating back to the sources of the Greek Magical Papyri.[33] The two manuscripts in which segments of rec. C appear along with some form of the *Magical Treatise*, Harley 5596 and Parisinus Graec. 2419, are also the *only* independent texts of the *Magical Treatise* to include some form of each and every ritual element seen in rec. C. Moreover, the fifteenth-century Harley manuscript is the earliest extant manuscript of the *Magical Treatise* to include *any* of those elements. Even the divinatory operations in the Harley *Magical Treatise* evince a deeper integration with the overall

---

33 On the three-day purification, see e.g. *PGM* III.282-409, IV.475-829, 1265-74, VII.319-34. The black-handled knife appears as early as the eleventh century in Rashi's commentary on the Babylonian Talmud, Sanhedrin 67b, in reference to an *onykhomanteia* or thumbnail scrying operation (Skinner, 2013: 303), and was still known in Greek folk magic of the early twentieth century, particularly in relation to dealings with fairies (Marathakis, 2011: 85, citing Politis, N. 1994. *Paradoseis: Meletai peri tou Biou kai tēs Glōssēs tou Hellēnikou Laou*. Athens: Grammata). Finally, Jackson (1988: 22 ff.) identifies a number of other allusions from the *TSol* corpus which bear comparison with material in the *PGM*.

ritual program and its relation to rec. C than may be superficially apparent: in addition to utilizing (albeit somewhat arbitrarily) the black-handled knife, the katoptromantic experiment culminates in summoning a hierarchy of spirits through the agency of one initially so conjured, learning their names, and commanding them to take an oath of obedience, all of which recapitulates key elements of the *TSol*, and rec. C in particular.

A number of evidentiary implications can be discerned in the above, from which several important inferences may be drawn: first, disparate segments of rec. C are correlated across two manuscripts composed perhaps a century apart with those *Magical Treatise* texts presenting a relatively cohesive ritual complex which appears to be adumbrated at various points in those same rec. C segments. This correlation supports the real unity of those segments as exemplars of a coherent text no longer extant in a complete form in any one manuscript; in other words, rec. C actually exists – it wasn't just a chimera cobbled together in Chester McCown's imagination. The intertextuality of rec. C and the *Magical Treatise* also suggests an editorial intent on the part of these manuscripts' redactors to represent something approaching a consistent ritual-magical theory through the independent elements they brought together, either with an eye towards the edification of posterity or simply for their own intellectual satisfaction. As to the relative place of these manuscripts within the history of Solomonic magical texts, we have in Harley 5596 a version of the *Magical Treatise* which is perhaps the earliest extant Greek text bearing a comprehensive Solomonic ritual rubric, the internal coherence of which has also been recognized by Stephen Skinner.[34] That ritual text is paired with a fragmentary (and thus necessarily antecedent) recension of the *TSol* describing an array of ritual paraphernalia not found in other versions of that narrative, which are also integral to the program of the ritual manual itself. It is my hypothesis, therefore,

34 Skinner, 2013: 104

that rec. C brought together a collection of traditional Hellenic magical methods and materia, along with a unique onomasticon of demons with whom to apply them, within a mythically-resonant narrative to form what would become a paradigm for the entire subsequent genre of the Solomonic grimoire.

Central to the interrogation of demons in the *TSol* tradition and certain parts of the *Magical Treatise* is the demand that they each divulge – and in rec. C, inscribe – their own names, as well as those of the angels or other powers by whom they are thwarted. In terms of methodological precedents, only two or three passages in all of the extant Greco-Egyptian Magical Papyri, to consider just one possible example, allude to any remotely similar procedure for identifying the beings with whom one is communicating.[35] Names and the act of naming are, of course, pervasive in the papyri, and absolutely indispensable to the invocatory theory of magical empowerment and command espoused therein, so perhaps it is for that very reason that there are so few instances in which the operator is not simply given the name of the god or *daimōn* in question as part of the ritual instructions. And if, as I suggest, rec. C finds itself heir to the same traditions of magical praxis that the Papyri record, then perhaps it should be no surprise that a voluminous index of such names forms the very centerpiece of the text!

---

35 *PGM* I.42-195, XIII.1-343, *PDM* xiv.528-53

A Note on the Translation

In translating this text from the original Greek, I have striven to produce a rendering that reads as relatively fluent modern English. As the primary purpose of this translation is to facilitate scholarly and practical consultation, I have erred toward a literal rather than literary interpretation wherever the text seemed to demand such a decision, leaving any deeper exegesis to the art of the reader. Likewise, words and passages which seem to permit more than one viable sense have been annotated with the original Greek, as have instances of apparent wordplay (which I attempt to preserve to some degree), and particularly uncertain readings (which are additionally indicated by '?'). This translation is primarily based upon the edition of the Greek text by McCown (1922), cross-referenced against photographic reproductions of the material in Harley MS 5596 and Parisinus Graec. MS 2419.

Concerning the names and their sigils, these two manuscripts evince so many similarities, as well as conflations and omissions that are clearly copyist's errors, that it is tempting to suppose that one served as model for the other (albeit under the hand of a rather inattentive scribe, or one who exercised a great deal of creative license). However, this hypothesis fails to account for a dozen or so sigils which bear no discernible resemblance between the Harley and Paris manuscripts, leaving open the possibility that each of these redactions derives from a separate exemplar and attesting to a surprising degree of heterogeneity within the manuscript tradition of a text as niche as this one particular recension of the *Testament of Solomon*. In any case, these onomastic and figural variants are annotated as to their originating manuscripts.

TESTAMENT OF SOLOMON

INCIPIT[36]

A testament of most wise Solomon with its parallel names[37] which were guarded as mysteries by Hezekiah after the death of David the King.

PROLOGUE

1. It came to be after the death of David the King, having prayed that his son would build Zion, and he himself also praying, there came a voice saying: "Solomon, son of David, the lord[38] god of your fathers himself having heard your prayers has given to you all power, and behold! You will come to see all the wisdom gleaming like snow before your face and eyes."

2. Having heard these things, and as though illuminated by that gleaming and inspired to the purpose, I began imploring and begging[39] god, speaking thus: "Eternal god", I said, "inconceivable[40] god, uncreated and invisible, having created everything by your spirit alone, behold the prayer of your slave and elucidate the works of your hands.

3. For just as you have done, god, making and sustaining in

---

36 Present in Bononiensis Uni. MS 3632 and Parisinus Graec. MS 2419

37 'with its parallel names' = μετά τῶν παραλλήλων αὐτῆς ὀνομάτων

38 'lord' = κύριος; this and Σαβαώθ 'Sabaōth' are the only epithets applied to θεός 'god' [which, according to McCown's edition, is not capitalized] in this recension, neither of which was exclusively Jewish or Christian in usage.

39 ' begging' = δεόμενος

40 ' inconceivable' = ἀπερινόητε

composition each of our bodies, the fruitbearing and non-fruitbearing trees, beasts and birds, so too the very divine air which all of nature breathes.

4. Your greatness is therefore secreted[41] where it may be laid open before my eyes and I may see your hidden wisdom, so that you will be blessed unto the ages; amen."

5. These vows being made, therefore, a voice was heard saying: "Solomon, Solomon, the lord god will say of you: 'He began the foundation of my house in the name of my heavenly Zion.'" And thus began the building of Zion.

IX[42]

8. And having said these things, he[43] then, weeping, said: "I implore you, king Solomon, not to burn me with the seal, and I promise you by an oath that in the name of Ontos[44] I will offer to you all the demons and will deliver these pawns to you by each one's signs as well as his powers and abilities and those over which he exercises authority." And I, Solomon, said: "If you will do this, you will be free."

9. And he said to me: "Take unborn black goats, 51 in number, and bring to me a new knife with three parts of black horn[45], and flay the goats."

41 ' secreted' = δυσωπῶ

42 Chapters I – IX.7 in manuscripts containing rec. C material generally correspond to other recensions upon which extant translations have been based; see Duling 1983.

43 A headless demon named Φονος 'Murder', previously introduced at IX.1-2.

44 Probably corresponding to Ornias in the other recensions, namely the demon who has been fetching the others for Solomon.

45 'with three parts of black horn' = τρίκωλον μελανοκέρατον

10. Then he commanded the required[46] human blood to be fetched for the skins and he recorded these upon two leaves and he wrote them in a triodion,[47] and each one found his name written in his own hand upon the skins as well as his sign and his working and his rulership thus:

X

1. Tzianphiel, *vel* Tzēanphiel[48]: rules 140; he[49] also works to report things past and things present and things that shall be.

HARLEY MS 5596   PARISINUS GRAEC. MS 2419

2. Pharan: rules 1000; he also works to fulfill all that one wills. He is also able to raise fire into the air and to bring down water and to point out stars.

HARLEY MS 5596   PARISINUS GRAEC. MS 2419

46 'required' ?= δευθῆναι; this participle stubbornly resisted positive identification, but I have conjectured that it is as an erroneous or archaic form of δεηθῆναι, aorist passive infinitive of δέω.

47 'triodion' = τριωδίω, i.e. an Eastern Orthodox Lenten liturgical book. McCown suggests this may have been an error for τριόδω, perhaps signifying 'in three ways'; nevertheless, the idea of blasphemously filling a triodion with this roster of demons, a quasi-liturgy in its own right, is in keeping with the sarcastic humor which seems to emerge sporadically in this and other recensions of the *TSol*.

48 Parisinus Graec. MS 2419

49 While I have, in the absence of indications to the contrary, arbitrarily gendered the demons as masculine, the *TSol* itself, in its various recensions, is interesting, if not unique, among works of Christian demonology in that it includes several explicitly feminine demons.

3. Machoumet[50]: rules 200; he works to make people[51] laugh at one another. And he also causes quadrupeds to speak like people and people to appear headless. He also causes these[52] to walk about naked, but also the irrational cattle[53] to see one another as wild beasts[54].

───∧───   ∧──√√

HARLEY MS 5596   PARISINUS GRAEC. MS 2419

50 *Sic!* The use of the name Μαχουμετ in this context likely reflects the pervasive medieval Christian conception of Muhammad as a false prophet and Islam as a kind of Christian heresy. Schwarz (2012: 12) notes that some early elements of the textual tradition that would become the *TSol* demonstrate a consciousness of active ideological rivalry between Christian-Jewish and pagan communities in late antiquity, evident in their demonization and subordination of figures drawn from pagan culture. A precisely analogous process can be observed in rec. C of the *TSol*, where our redactor, working in the fifteenth century, has included the Prophet of Islam among the demons enumerated in the text's catalogue. Whether composed in southern Italy (McCown, 1922: 111), or elsewhere in the Hellenophone world, and whether in the context of the fall of Constantinople to the Ottomans or to the Fourth Crusade (see Marathakis, 2011: 75), the empire of Islam would have loomed large as a very real political, military, and religious rival to Christendom in the mind of a Greek author. The symbols of Islam – perhaps foremost among them its Prophet – invested thus with the force of an existential and spiritual threat, became susceptible to literal demonization and magically-imposed subjugation by demonologically-inclined partisans of the Byzantine cause.

51 I translate ἀνθρώπους etc. as the more accurate 'people' rather than the archaic, if flavorful, 'men'.

52 Presumably the aforementioned people.

53 'cattle' = κτήνη; 'beasts', but with the connotation of domestication.

54 'wild beasts' = θηρία ἄγρια; perhaps thereby causing instinctual fear and panic amongst them.

34

4. Napour: rules 50; he is able in one hour to provide gold and silver by means of which to satisfy your biological needs[55] in the meantime, and likewise clothes that are not shabby.[56]

HARLEY MS 5596   PARISINUS GRAEC. MS 2419

5. Rhoapt: rules 400; he also works to make one become wise and implants understanding.

HARLEY MS 5596   PARISINUS GRAEC. MS 2419

6. Parel, *vel* Parelkoziou[57]: rules 25; he also works to make trees bloom despite the season, and also brings forth new growth in dry wood.

HARLEY MS 5596   PARISINUS GRAEC. MS 2419
sigil missing

7. Asmodeō, *vel* Asmōdeō,[58] Asmodeos[59]: rules 60; he is able to cause snow and rain in the summer, but also provides cherries in winter.

HARLEY MS 5596   PARISINUS GRAEC. MS 2419

---

55 'to satisfy your biological needs' = πρός τῆς απαντῆς σου τῆς ζωῆς καί τῆς γεννήσεως
56 'clothes that are not shabby' = στολάς μή ῥηγνυμενας
57 Harley MS 5596
58 Parisinus Graec. MS 2419
59 Harley MS 5596

8. Bēlet[60]: rules 200; she is able to bring about what one wills concerning Palestine.[61]

HARLEY MS 5596	PARISINUS GRAEC. MS 2419
entry absent	

9. Lasarak: rules 300; he is able to cause wars and the marshaling of troops and victories and acts of valor.

HARLEY MS 5596	PARISINUS GRAEC. MS 2419

10. Rhaamet, *vel* Raimet[62]: rules 200; this one foretells things to come and gives wealth.

HARLEY MS 5596	PARISINUS GRAEC. MS 2419

11. Tzerepones, *vel* Tzerepōnes[63]: rules 150; he is able to produce and arrange histories and images, and also to understand the voices of birds.

HARLEY MS 5596	PARISINUS GRAEC. MS 2419

60 'Bēlet' = Μπηλετ; for the historical evolution of Greek orthography see Horrocks (2010) and Arvaniti (1999).

61 Concerning this demon's name, gender, and geographic remit, see Appendix B.

62 Harley MS 5596

63 Parisinus Graec. MS 2419

12. Darōgan,[64] *vel* Itarogan[65]: rules 300; he also works to purify all pollution and to make the poor like the rich, and if it is up to him, to live like kings.

HARLEY MS 5596   PARISINUS GRAEC. MS 2419

13. Pelōn: rules 1000; he also works to betray castles and cities and countries.

HARLEY MS 5596   PARISINUS GRAEC. MS 2419

14. Soupiel: rules 1000; he also works to cause uprising against the tyrant and gives away government to another ruler and frees prisoners in prisons and likewise captives.

HARLEY MS 5596   PARISINUS GRAEC. MS 2419

15. Oriens: rules 500 spirits of the east; he himself is also able to do whatsoever all of these can.

HARLEY MS 5596   PARISINUS GRAEC. MS 2419

64 'Darōgan' = Νταρωγαν; see Horrocks (2010) and Arvaniti (1999).
65 Harley MS 5596

16. Amemōn: rules 500 southern[66] spirits; he himself can also do the same as these.

HARLEY MS 5596   PARISINUS GRAEC. MS 2419
sigil missing

17. Eltzēn, *vel* Eltzin[67]: rules 500 northern spirits; he himself can also do the same as these.

HARLEY MS 5596   PARISINUS GRAEC. MS 2419
sigil missing

18. Panōn: this one also rules 600 of the spirits of the sea; and he himself also works concerning winds and boats.

HARLEY MS 5596   PARISINUS GRAEC. MS 2419
sigil illegible

19. Boul: this one also rules 500 spirits of the west; he himself can also do the same as these.

HARLEY MS 5596   PARISINUS GRAEC. MS 2419
entry absent

---

66 'southern' = μεσημβρινῶν, also possibly 'midday'.
67 Harley MS 5596

20. Ampatzout: this one also rules 1000; he also works concerning every craft and learning and practical wisdom and literacy.

HARLEY MS 5596   PARISINUS GRAEC. MS 2419

21. Astarōth: rules 2000; he also works concerning those who depart and go away as well as those who stay. And he also causes treasures to be revealed.

HARLEY MS 5596   PARISINUS GRAEC. MS 2419

22. Loupēt: rules 5000; he also works concerning obeying and commanding and practicing, foundation and ruination and observation[68] and transferring from place to place.

HARLEY MS 5596   PARISINUS GRAEC. MS 2419

23. Apolēn, *vel* Apolii[69]: rules 100; he also works concerning enrichment and provides much gold and silver.

HARLEY MS 5596   PARISINUS GRAEC. MS 2419
                                 sigil illegible

---

68 'obeying and commanding and practicing, foundation and ruination and observation'
= ακούειν καί κράτειν καί πράττειν, κτίζειν καί χαλᾶν καί βλέπειν
69 Harley MS 5596

24. Asterōth,[70] vel "the other Astarōth"[71]: rules 1[72]; he also works concerning kingdoms and cities and castles and towers and buildings.

HARLEY MS 5596   PARISINUS GRAEC. MS 2419
sigil illegible

25. Latzēpher, *vel* Latzipher[73]: rules 3000; he works concerning all the rulers;[74] and namely the kings, and he is also able to do whatsoever is desired.

HARLEY MS 5596   PARISINUS GRAEC. MS 2419

26. Magōt, *vel* Magot[75]: he himself also rules 4000; he also works concerning speeches and deeds.

HARLEY MS 5596   PARISINUS GRAEC. MS 2419

70 Not to be confused with the aforementioned Astarōth.

71 'the other Astarōth' = ὁ ἕτερος ασταρωθ; Harley MS 5596

72 Possibly an error in McCown's edition for 1000 or 10,000; the notation in Harley MS 5596 is ambiguous.

73 Harley MS 5596

74 Emending McCown's edition to correct what seems almost certainly to be a semicolon mistaken for a period; cf. Harley MS 5596.

75 Parisinus Graec. MS 2419

27. Karap: rules 7000; he also works concerning cities and castles and households.

HARLEY MS 5596

PARISINUS GRAEC. MS 2419

28. Ouleos, *vel* Oulatos[76]: rules one tribe, or 10,000. He also brings about greatness and splendid clothes and games and false visions,[77] and makes asses of people and other animals such as you wish.

HARLEY MS 5596

PARISINUS GRAEC. MS 2419

29. Krinel: rules 200,000; he also works to kill men and women, and to bring about disputes and disturbances[78] and riots.

HARLEY MS 5596

PARISINUS GRAEC. MS 2419

30. Tougel: rules 600; he also brings about love, cities unto cities and people with people and men with women.

HARLEY MS 5596

PARISINUS GRAEC. MS 2419

76 Harley MS 5596
77 'false visions' = παροφθαλμίας
78 'disputes and disturbances' = μάχας καί ταραχάς

31. Setariel: rules 20; he reveals treasures, and also makes the use thereof unseen, observed by no one. And he also provides good judgment to women.

HARLEY MS 5596   PARISINUS GRAEC. MS 2419

32. Phakanel: rules 70,000; he also does all of the errands one wishes.

HARLEY MS 5596   PARISINUS GRAEC. MS 2419

33. Oel: rules 3000; and he himself is also able to do alone whatsoever all these can do.

HARLEY MS 5596   PARISINUS GRAEC. MS 2419

34. Lenel, *vel* Nenel,[79] Oelēnēl[80]: rules 30; he also works to provide gold and silver; and he brings forth women observed by no one.

HARLEY MS 5596   PARISINUS GRAEC. MS 2419
                       sigil partially illegible

79 Parisinus Graec. MS 2419
80 Harley MS 5596

35. Saratiel: rules 100; he also works concerning lunatics; and he is also reputed to make the moon descend.

HARLEY MS 5596   PARISINUS GRAEC. MS 2419

36. Myratziel, *vel* Miratzēel,[81] Myrakiel[82]: rules 20,000; he also works concerning warfare and laying siege and cities taken captive.

HARLEY MS 5596   PARISINUS GRAEC. MS 2419

37. Sansōniel, *vel* Sansoniel[83]: rules 7300; he also works to make great waves and violent winds.

HARLEY MS 5596   PARISINUS GRAEC. MS 2419

38. Asiel: rules 100,000; he works to reveal thefts and thieves and treasures which, though their location is well known, the part of that locale in which they lie is not.

HARLEY MS 5596   PARISINUS GRAEC. MS 2419

81 Parisinus Graec. MS 2419
82 Harley MS 5596
83 Harley MS 5596

39. Kastiel, *vel* Astiel[84]: rules 200; he also works to heal every infirmity.

HARLEY MS 5596

PARISINUS GRAEC. MS 2419

40. Meinget, *vel* Mingot[85]: rules 60; he is able to make serpents and dragons.

HARLEY MS 5596

PARISINUS GRAEC. MS 2419

41. Enodas: rules 50; he is able to conduct fire up into the air and to make chariots[86] appear to burn up.

HARLEY MS 5596

PARISINUS GRAEC. MS 2419

42. Atanianous, *vel* Antinianos[87]: rules 1000; he is able to give every craft and knowledge and understanding to people.

HARLEY MS 5596

PARISINUS GRAEC. MS 2419
sigil illegible

84 Harley MS 5596
85 Harley MS 5596
86 'chariots' = ἅρματα, i.e. military vehicles
87 Harley MS 5596

43. Myragkous, *vel* Miragkous,[88] Myrakos[89]: rules 30; he is able to command the sun not to appear.

HARLEY MS 5596   PARISINUS GRAEC. MS 2419

44. Potzeties, *vel* Potzetios[90]: rules 200; he is able to make people and animals rise into the air.

HARLEY MS 5596   PARISINUS GRAEC. MS 2419

45. Anet[91]: rules 100; he also makes known everything about stones and pearls and other metals.

HARLEY MS 5596   PARISINUS GRAEC. MS 2419

88 Parisinus Graec. MS 2419

89 Harley MS 5596

90 Harley MS 5596

91 The possibility of an etymological relation between the warlike north-west Semitic goddess Anat and the present demon, Anet – to say nothing of the vectors by which such a transmission may have occurred – raises questions which, while intriguing, are beyond the scope of the present study to pursue. Anat is known primarily from the Ugaritic textual corpus, and is not explicitly referred to in the Hebrew Bible, ענת appearing only as an element of the place name Beth Anat in Joshua 19:38 and Judges 1:33, and the personal name Shamgar ben Anat in Judges 3:31 (van der Toorn, 1999: 36-7).

46. Paltaphōte, *vel* Paltaphate[92]: rules 100,000; he makes known all the plants and in what manner each is effective and beneficial.

HARLEY MS 5596

PARISINUS GRAEC. MS 2419

47. Saparatzēl, *vel* Sapatēl[93]: rules 50; he makes known all the birds and in what manner each is effective.

HARLEY MS 5596

PARISINUS GRAEC. MS 2419

48. Tarseus: rules 60; he also makes known the trees and in what manner each is effective.

HARLEY MS 5596

PARISINUS GRAEC. MS 2419

49. Nabel, *vel* Nabal[94]: rules 40; he also makes known all the quadrupeds and in what manner each is beneficial.

HARLEY MS 5596

PARISINUS GRAEC. MS 2419

92 Harley MS 5596
93 Harley MS 5596
94 Harley MS 5596

50. Sataēl, *vel* Tasaēl[95]: rules 5[96]; he works concerning crocodiles and puts them into submission.

HARLEY MS 5596   PARISINUS GRAEC. MS 2419

51. Napalaikon, *vel* Nampalaikon[97]: rules 5; he is able to make the day night and the night day.

HARLEY MS 5596   PARISINUS GRAEC. MS 2419
                        sigil illegible

52. Makatak, *vel* Makkatak[98]: rules 5; he also works concerning the increase of flocks and horses.

HARLEY MS 5596   PARISINUS GRAEC. MS 2419

53. And I deposited this great and divine mystery in a secret place forsaken by my children, having delivered an oath by god Sabaōth of holy name to impart it no more to anyone, but in a secure place to keep it as a treasure unspent; these oaths unseen and unknown by the masses during the terrible exile.[99]

95 Harley MS 5596

96 Parisinus Graec. MS 2419 ascribes Sataēl and the two succeeding demons, Napalaikon and Makatak, 5000 subordinates rather than 5.

97 Harley MS 5596

98 Parisinus Graec. MS 2419

99 'exile' = ἀπεχώρισα, perhaps a metatextual (or, in the pseudepigraphic context, 'prophetic') reference to the Jewish captivity in Babylon and/or post-70 CE diaspora.

XI

1. And Beelzeboul, whom Entzianphiel[100] summoned for me, was asked if there are also female demons, of which claim is also made, as have been purported to be seen.

2. And departing, this one brought before me the one called Onoskelis, beauteous in form with the body of a fine-skinned woman, but the shins[101] of a mule.

3. And she having come, I spoke to her saying: "Who are you?" And she said to me: "I am called Onoskelis, an embodied[102] spirit. And I lurk upon the earth; I dwell in a cave where gold lies.

4. And I have a many-faceted character: whereas sometimes I choke people like a noose, other times I pervert them from their innermost[103] nature.

5. Many are my dwellings; and also I frequently associate with the people to whom I am like a woman, and foremost the honey-complexioned, for they are also of my constellation; for they also make obeisance to my star both clandestinely and conspicuously."

6. And I, Solomon, asked her: "Whence were you born?" and she

---

100 sic; cf. Tzianphiel at X.1

101 'shins' = κνήμας; McCown's text has the nonsensical κτήμας 'properties', but he indicates the correct word in a footnote.

102 'embodied' = σεσωματοποιημένον, literally 'made into a body'

103 'innermost' = επιεγκόνων; McCown suggests a derivation from επι+εν+χωνω, which can plausibly be interpreted as 'most in-buried'.

said: "From the sound of Bathsheba whinnying like a horse."[104]

7.[105] And I shut her away beneath four great stones. And she cried out: "Let me out, let me out, and I will bring to you a table with a bowl and chalice, whosoever grasping will be lashed with whips all over, offering to surrender the edibles[106] and drinks to you."

8. And commanding that she be fetched, she brought to me a stone table of jasper; its length four cubits and width four cubits, and having among the horns[107] four ant-lions speaking when prompted by me as much as I wish.

9. And having now called it to hand and the table having been brought I sought also the chalice, and yet a chalice of luminous[108]

104 'From the sound of Bathsheba whinnying like a horse' = ἀπό φωνῆς βηρσαβεὲ ἱππικῆς χρηματικῆς, reading χρηματικῆς as a conjugated form of χρεμετιζειν, and ἱππικῆς = ἵππος + genitive adjectival suffix -ικης.

105 The perplexing vignette played out in XI.7-9 shares a number of details and structural elements with a particular tradition of divination found from the Demotic Magical Papyri down to collections of magical methods contemporaneous with rec. C itself. In PDM xiv.528-53, a 'vessel inquiry', Anubis is ordered to bring in a table, wine jar, and bread for the entertainment of the other gods to whom the operator will pose questions. This is strikingly similar to another divinatory operation utilizing a water vessel found in manuscripts A, P4, and B of the *Magical Treatise*, as well as a *katoptromanteia* in manuscripts H and B2 (See Marathakis, 2011 for details of the manuscripts), the latter of which (i.e. Bononiensis Uni. MS 3632) preserves the relevant passage of rec. C as well. A material, rather than phantasmal, table with dishes and food also serves as the locus for binding and interrogating a demon or ghost in manuscripts B, B2, B3, and fragmentarily in A. It may be conjectured that the sequence wherein Onoskelis is compelled to furnish such a table so that Solomon can engage in some strange discourse with its occupants represents a confused conflation – if not a deliberate parody – of these ancient divinatory methods.

106 'edibles' ?= βρωτὰ

107 'horns' ?= κέρασιν; possibly suggesting a horned altar like that described in Exodus 27:2.

108 'luminous' ?= λυχνίτην

stone and containing a dedicated[109] form, and whereas the table furnished ever so much food, I sought for the chalice to supply so much to drink.

XII

1. Therefore I sought out by means of the seal Paltiel Tzamal, and at once presenting himself he said to me: "Solomon, son of David, why do you test your slaves, male and female?[110] We all serve and promise to submit and to hold in surety our names that we have written and every one of the powers having been announced for all of your days.[111]

2. Which safekeeping the one so commanded fulfills most readily. And we implore you not to allow us to go away into a vast sea."[112]

3. And I asked him if there is resurrection of the dead. And he cried a great cry saying: "There is, there is, by the mighty and living god. For we are also of the opinion that there persist damned[113] ones who were formerly luminous, and yet they do not incline themselves to repentance.

4. And I say these things to you, O King, god is one alone, who is thrice praised by the luminous angels. He therefore handed us over to you, and we household servants put in order and handed over our names and likewise our seals.

---

109 'dedicated' ?= επιδέδωκεν

110 'your slaves, male and female' = τούς δούλους σου καί τὰς δούλας σου

111 'for all of your days' = ἕως καιροῦ σου

112 This apparent non sequitur is almost certainly a paraphrase of the demons' supplication in Luke 8:31, in the story of the Gerasene demoniac.

113 'damned' = εζοφώθημεν, literally 'having come to darkness'

5. And whoever, O King, learns the truth, purifies himself for three days and one of us seized by that ruler is called into the joint of his hand to fulfill his command, and just as a household slave is obedient to his own master, so likewise is one thus called also to our names you have acquired.

6. These names, then, must be chosen[114] by means of a jasper stone inscribed with the twelve zodiac signs; and amidst the snake and wolf, mast[115] and bear, and over the drum bearing a chalice, from the top of this these letters also: ZABAPΖHC, and at once we are subjected to your acquisition and without freedom of will.[116]

XIII

1. Except, O King, we also offer this to you: many people intend to seek such a great mystery as this in order to subject us to themselves, and if you will hear us we will speak." And I said: "Speak, rebels and deceivers."

2. And he said: "Leave you to your descendants alone the treasure and not to the masses and the naive. And make of us a sign such that after you have died Hezekiah the King will make another

114 'chosen' = επιλέγειν

115 'mast' = ιστός, also possibly 'web' or 'loom'; perhaps a constituent constellation of Argo Navis?

116 The inscription of complex figurative images along with an apparent *nomen barbarum* upon a semiprecious stone is highly suggestive of the methods prescribed throughout the Greek Magical Papyri for fashioning talismanic rings. For the use of a jasper stone in particular, though not specifically pertaining to the summoning or command of spirits, see PGM V.447-58; XII.201-69, 270-350. The transmission of this particular *materia magica* persisted within the Solomonic tradition well into the period of early modern grimoires, appearing alongside virgin parchment and magnetic stone as a suitable medium for the creation of a talisman or pentacle in the *Clavicula Salomonis* preserved in the 18th-century Wellcome MS 4670.

testament unto the world and this one will be hidden and not apparent to the common and naive, so that the treasure is not abandoned to the inhabitants of the earth.[117]

3. For no one from the beginning until today has enslaved us, nor conceded that we obey mortal bodies.

4. For whereas Hezekiah, O King, will burn much of his patrimony and obliterate many other writings, thus he will also fortify the civilized world[118] and terminate the superfluous.

5. And I, Solomon, having listened said this: "I bind you into the unshakeable throne of god and into the birds that go about above one's head so that you tell me by which angel all things are abolished."[119]

6. And he said to me: "King Solomon, we are all abolished by the power of god and in the name Agla,[120] but since you alone bound us by the seal we are subdued until a certain point.

7. For there will come days in which many are winnowed,[121] and during this we will plead on your behalf so that in generations to come we will bear a memorial[122] of your kingship and commend this to Hezekiah the king so that it will have been demonstrated and spread throughout the world that we will

---

117 'inhabitants of the earth' = τοῖς οἰκουμένοις

118 'the civilized world' = τὴν οἰκουμένην

119 'I bind you into the unshakeable throne of god and into the birds that go about above one's head so that you tell me by which angel all things are abolished' = ἐξορκίζω σε εἰς τόν θρόνον τοῦ θεοῦ τό ἀσάλευτον καί εἰς τό ὄρνεον τό περιπετόμενον ἐπάνω τῆς κεφαλῆς αὐτοῦ ἵνα με εἴπης ἐν ποίῳ ἀγγέλῳ οἱ πάντες καταργεῖσθε

120 'Agla' = Ἀγλά, presumably transliterating the Hebrew acronym אגלא

121 'winnowed' = δηθήσῃ

122 'memorial' = σημεῖον

present to him a new testament.

8. And this one, in which we have truthfully inscribed our names, he will burn up as well without a single one preserved, in expectation of the new advent[123] of god having become widespread.

9. And because Hezekiah had been given this[124] by us it will be handed over to the whole world, and like some great treasure preserved by the wise, will be issued into the world like a plaything and a fraud.

10. Having heard these things I, Solomon, prayed to god and said: "God of the fathers, great Adonai, who has granted wisdom to your slave, reveal to me that which must be done."

11. And there came a voice saying: "Solomon, Solomon, cede to Hezekiah a booklet,[125] having sealed away the seal itself."[126]

12. And taking a seat I wrote: "To Hezekiah the future King: King Solomon, son of David, dispatched to you the following. Take from Paltiel Tzamal a testament which he will give to you and to the enrichment of the whole world; and I have consigned that of my own to fire except for one which also shall be stamped in letters in stone[127] as long as the great and mighty should wish."

---

123 'new advent' = παρουσία πάλιν

124 i.e. the new, spurious testament referred to in XIII.7

125 'booklet' = γραμμάτιον

126 'having sealed away the seal itself' = τῇ σφραγῖδι ταύτη εκσφραγισάμενος

127 'stone' = λαΐνεοις, an evidently rare form, attested e.g. in Euripides *Phoenissae* l. 115

13. These things having been written were entrusted to Tzamal, and again I asked him if there is a good person in the world to whom, being sound in body and unblemished, riches shall be granted. And he said to me: "Only one in the midst of the earth shall be granted such by trivial letters of your own script."

14. And just so, taking a seat I wrote in Chaldaean[128] letters by my own hand for the one sound in body and unblemished to whom riches shall be granted, handing over only Palestine, which, whensoever it will be revealed, had not been acquired alone but also all the people[129] enjoying health and those who are wealthy offering gifts always, since these came down from heaven in the hands of the Most High, possessing the handiwork of great glories, which they have endowed to me as well.

15. Thus am I, Solomon. And in perpetuity mighty god, Most High Sabaōth: amen.

EXPLICIT[130]

End of the testament of most wise Solomon, son of David, which being recorded after the death of David the King was preserved by Hezekiah the King. It was written down by I, John, a doctor of aro:[131] in the year 6949, indiction 4,[132] in the month of December, the 14th. And god is with us and none against us.

---

128 'Chaldaean' = χαλδαϊκοῖς. Bononiensis Uni. MS 3632 includes an illustration apparently representing this 'Chaldaean' writing, captioned thus: 'this is the stamp which Solomon displayed over his vessel' = ἀυτ(η) ἡ βουλ(α) ἥν εφορεσ(ε) σωλομον επανο τη σκευει αυτου

129 'the people' = κόσμον, Italiot dialect form of κόσμος

130 Present in Bononiensis Uni. MS 3632

131 'aro' = αρο; possibly an abbreviation of the patronymic Aron, or an unidentified toponym

132 This date corresponds to the Gregorian year 1440 (McCown, 1922: 23-4)

A. Manuscript Representations of the Seal of Solomon

*Text accompanying the seal of Solomon
depicted in Harley MS 5596 f. 8v:*

'And the seal said this: behold this is the seal:' = Ἡ δε σφραγις ταυτα ελεγεν: ιδου αὐτη εστιν ἡ σφραγις: [the inscription depicted in the illustration of the seal, in the scribe's idiosyncratic blend of miniscule and uncial script, reads: κ ο θ λ ρ σ β ι ω ν κ α ω α ω ε λ ι Γ ω ι σ C Γ ω α α ε σ ρ ȣ ρ]

Text concerning the seal(s) of Solomon depicted in Bononiensis Uni. MS 3632 and Parisinus Graec. MS 2419, as redacted by McCown from ibid.:

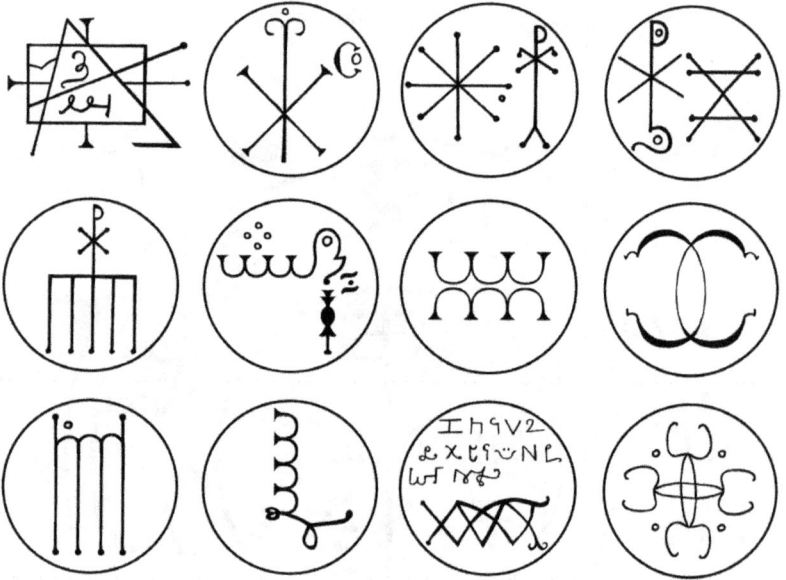

'And the inscription of the seal of the ring was this:' = Ἦν δὲ ἡ ἐπιγραφὴ τῆς σφραγῖδος τοῦ δακτυλίου αὕτη: [the image (see Parisinus Graec. MS 2419, f.139) depicts twelve seals, one or all of which were evidently engraved on the ring] 'and he gave it to Solomon; these are those eleven seals which the angel gave with the twelve stones; from among which the one seal holds the power of grace.' = καί ἔδωκεν τῷ Σολομῶντι; αὕταί εἰσιν αἱ ἔνδεκα σφραγῖδαι ἃς ἔδωκεν ὁ ἄγγελος μετὰ τῶν δώδεκα λίθων; ἐξ ὧν ἡ μία σφραγῖδα ἔχει τῶν χαρισμάτων τό μέγεθος.

B. Concerning Μπηλετ / Bēlet / B'lt

Based upon the historical phonological-orthographic work of Amalia Arvaniti and Geoffrey Horrocks,[133] I am reasonably satisfied that 'Bēlet' is an accurate romanization of Μπηλετ as pronounced in medieval Byzantine Greek. In addition, the instructions for consecrating virgin parchment in the text of the *Magical Treatise* which shares Harley MS 5596 with the segment of rec. C in which Μπηλετ is found includes amidst an invocation of divine names the phrase μπαρουχ, αττα, αδωναι, which Marathakis observes is an apparent corruption of 'Baruch atah Adonai',[134] a common element of Jewish liturgical blessings; this demonstrates that this manuscript was indeed written in a dialect of Greek in which Μπ = /b/.

The name Bēlet bears a striking phonological similarity to the West Semitic *B'lt*, 'Mistress' or 'Lady', a name or epithet of several ancient Near-Eastern goddessess, most notably the tutelary deity of Phoenician Byblos, *B'lt gbl*.[135] I would be inclined to pass over this similarity as mere coincidence, were it not for the fact that the text of rec. C explicitly associates Μπηλετ's remit with precisely the historical geographic region, Palestine, to which *B'lt* belonged. This suggests that the late-medieval Byzantine author of this entry, or his source, retained at least some superficial awareness of this particular Bronze-Age Phoenician cult, most likely from the account by Sanchuniathon transmitted via Philo and Eusebius. In Philo's Greek 'translation' of a euhemeristic Phoenician theogony purportedly composed by one Sanchuniathon, extant only in

---

133 Arvaniti, 1999; Horrocks, 2010
134 Marathakis, 2011: 159 n. 1
135 van der Toorn, 1999: 139

paraphrase in the *Προπαρασκευης Ευαγγελικης* (*Preparation for the Gospel*) of Eusebius, θεα Βααλτιδι receives the city of Byblos from Kronos.[136] As her name here is in the dative case, it can be deduced that the nominative form is simply Βααλτις, which can in turn be parsed as a transliteration of the Semitic *B'lt* with the Greek feminine noun- and adjective-forming suffix -ις. While it is attested as a place name, בעלת *ba'ălāt*, in Joshua 19:44, 1 Kings 9:18, and 2 Chronicles 8:6, no form of *B'lt* appears as a divine name or title in the Hebrew Bible.[137] It seems at least quite probable, then, that Philo, by way of Eusebius's popular work of Christian apologetics, was the vector by which this ancient Phoenician goddess, at least in name, came to late medieval Byzantium.

As Skinner has noted, the gods as presented in the Greek Magical Papyri are often "...delegated to the same level of functionality as their daimones.... The gods in the papyri were treated in much the same way as they were in later Greek folk religion, as useful, but almost daimonic, tricksy and dangerous".[138] In the late-medieval context of the *TSol* even moreso than the relatively syncretistic environment of the PGM, the pattern of degrading – indeed, literally demonizing – alien divinities is unmistakable.

The next-earliest attestation of a grimoire spirit with a *B'lt*-form name that I have been able to locate is Bylet, in the fifteenth-century Bayerische Staatsbibliothek MS CLM 849, where it is evidently no more than a scribal error for Lylet, i.e. Lilith,[139] disqualifying at least that text as a vector for propagating the etymology of Μπηλετ into the later grimoire tradition.

136 *Preaparationis Evangelicae* I.10.35
137 van der Toorn, 1999: 139-40
138 Skinner, 2013: 63
139 Kieckhefer, 1998: 106

BIBLIOGRAPHY

PRIMARY SOURCES, AND EDITIONS THEREOF

Ashmand, J.M. (trans). 1822. *Ptolemy's Tetrabiblos.* Internet Sacred Text Archive, http://www.sacred-texts.com/astro/ptb/index.htm

Betz, H.D. (ed). 1986. *The Greek Magical Papyri in Translation, Including the Demotic Spells.* Chicago: University of Chicago Press.

Boudet, J.-P. 2003. Les who's who démonologiques de la Renaissance et leurs ancêtres médiévaux. *Médiévales* 44: 117-40.

Dindorfius, G. (ed). 1867. *Preaparationis Evangelicae, Libri I-X.* Lipsiae: B.G. Teubneri.

Duling, D.C. (trans). 1983. Testament of Solomon. In James H. Charlesworth (ed), *The Old Testament Pseudepigrapha – Volume I: Apocalyptic Literature and Testaments*, pp. 935-87. Garden City: Doubleday & Company, Inc.

Harley MS 5596. British Library Digitised Manuscripts, http://www.bl.uk/manuscripts/FullDisplay.aspx?ref=Harley_MS_5596

Harms, D. and Peterson, J.H. (eds). 2015. *Book of magic, with instructions for invoking spirits, etc. (ca. 1577-1583)* – Folger SHAKESPEARE LIBRARY manuscript V.b.26. Esoteric Archives, http://www.esotericarchives.com/folger/v_b_26_transcription.pdf

Marathakis, I. (ed, trans). 2011. *The Magical Treatise of Solomon or* Hygromanteia. Singapore: Golden Hoard Press.

McCown, C.C. (ed). 1922. *The Testament of Solomon.* Leipzig: J.C. Hinrichs'sche Buchhandlung.

Parisinus Graec. MS 2419. Bibliothèque Nationale de France, https://gallica.bnf.fr/ark:/12148/btv1b10723580f

Peterson, J. (ed). 2009. *Liber Juratus Honorii or The Sworne Booke of Honorius.* Esoteric Archives, http://www.esotericarchives. com/juratus/juratus.htm

Skinner, S. (ed). 2010. Marcus Collisson (trans), *Psellus' Dialogue on the Operation of Daemons.* Singapore: Golden Hoard Press.

SECONDARY LITERATURE

Alexander, L. and Harding, J. 1999. Dating the Testament of Solomon. University of St Andrews, https://www.st-andrews. ac.uk/divinity/rt/otp/guestlectures/harding/

Arvaniti, A. 1999. Standard Modern Greek. *Journal of the International Phonetic Association* 29.2: 167-72.

Duffy, J. 1995. Reactions of Two Byzantine Intellectuals to the Theory and Practice of Magic: Michael Psellos and Michael Italikos. In Henry Maguire (ed), *Byzantine Magic*, pp. 83-97. Washington, D.C.: Dumbarton Oaks Research Library and Collection.

Duling, D.C. 1988. The Testament of Solomon: Retrospect and Prospect. *Journal for the Study of the Pseudepigrapha* 1.2: 87-112.

Horrocks, G. 2010. *Greek: A History of the Language and its Speakers*, second edition. Chichester: Wiley-Blackwell.

Jackson, H.M. 1988. Notes on the Testament of Solomon. *Journal for the Study of Judaism* 19.1: 19-60.

Kieckhefer, R. 1998. *Forbidden Rites: A Necromancer's Manual of the Fifteenth Century*. University Park: Pennsylvania State University Press.

O'Neill, S. 2017. The Demonic Body: Demonic Ontology and the Domicile of the Demons in Apuleius and Augustine. In Benjamin W. McCraw and Robert Arp (eds), *Philosophical Approaches to Demonology*, pp. 39-58. New York: Routledge.

Schwarz, S.L. 2007. Reconsidering the *Testament of Solomon*. *Journal for the Study of the Pseudepigrapha* 16.3: 203-37.

Schwarz, S.L. 2012. Demons and Douglas: Applying Grid and Group to the Demonologies of the *Testament of Solomon*. *Journal of the American Academy of Religion* 80.4: 1-23.

Skinner, S. 2013. *Magical Techniques and Implements present in Graeco-Egyptian Magical Papyri, Byzantine Greek Solomonic Manuscripts and European Grimoires: Transmission, Continuity and Commonality* Unpublished PhD thesis, University of Newcastle.

van der Toorn, K., et al (eds). 1999. *Dictionary of Deities and Demons in the Bible*, second edition. Boston: Brill.

www.ingramcontent.com/pod-product-compliance
Lightning Source LLC
Chambersburg PA
CBHW051434090426
42737CB00014B/2965